Great White Sharks

by Leighton Taylor

Lerner Publications Company • Minneapolis

To the students, teachers, and staff of the Pt. Dume Marine Science Elementary School, Malibu, California

The photographs in this book are used with permission of: © Randy Faris/CORBIS, p. 4; © Brandon Cole/Visuals Unlimited, pp. 6, 10, 11, 13, 15, 16, 20, 24, 27, 38, 43, 46-47; © age fotostock/SuperStock, pp. 7, 21, 22, 23, 31; © Caterina Gennaro Kurr/SeaPics.com, p. 8; © Saul Gonor/SeaPics.com, p. 9; © James D. Watt/SeaPics.com, p. 12; © Marty Snyderman/Visuals Unlimited, pp. 14, 19; © Jeffrey L. Rotman/CORBIS, pp. 17, 34, 40; © Bob Cranston/SeaPics.com, p. 18; © C & M Fallows/SeaPics.com, p. 25; © Greg Huglin/SuperStock, p. 26; © Mike Parry/ Minden Pictures, p. 28; © Ralf Kiefner/SeaPics.com, p. 29; © Klaus Jost- www.jostimages.com, pp. 30, 32; © Brad Sheard/SuperStock, p. 33; © Stephen Frink/CORBIS, p. 35; © Leighton Taylor, p. 36; © PhotoDisc Royalty Free by Getty Images, p. 37; © James D. Watt/ SeaPics.com, p. 39; © Mauritius/SuperStock, p. 41; © Peter Lane Taylor/Visuals Unlimited, p. 42.

Front cover: © James D.Watt/SeaPics.com

Lerner Publications Company
A division of Lerner Publishing Group
241 First Avenue North
Minneapolis, MN 55401 U.S.A.

Website address: www.lernerbooks.com

Library of Congress Cataloging-in-Publication Data

Taylor, L. R. (Leighton R.)
    Great white sharks / by Leighton Taylor.
       p. cm. — (Early bird nature books)
    Includes index.
    ISBN-13: 978-0-8225-2868-5 (lib. bdg. : alk. paper)
    ISBN-10: 0-8225-2868-1 (lib. bdg. : alk. paper)
    1. White shark—Juvenile literature. I. Title. II. Series.
QL638.95.L3T39 2006
597.3'3—dc22   2005004337

Manufactured in the United States of America
1 2 3 4 5 6 – JR – 11 10 09 08 07 06

Contents

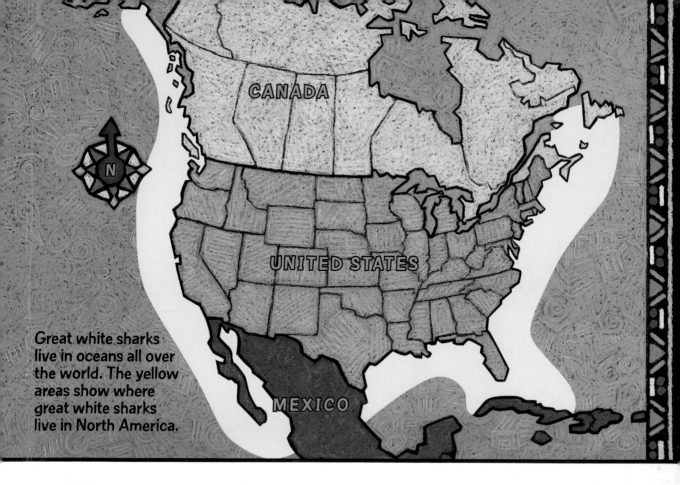

Great white sharks live in oceans all over the world. The yellow areas show where great white sharks live in North America.

CANADA

UNITED STATES

MEXICO

Be a Word Detective

Can you find these words as you read about the great white shark's life? Be a detective and try to figure out what they mean. You can turn to the glossary on page 46 for help.

bands	**gills**	**prey**
compete	**litter**	**pups**
dorsal fins	**pectoral fins**	**serrated**
endangered	**pores**	**streamlined**
fossils	**predators**	

Chapter 1

This is a great white shark. How many kinds of sharks are there?

The Great White Shark

Sharks are swift and sleek. They speed through the water. They swim quickly to hunt down fish, seals, and sea lions.

There are more than 350 species, or kinds, of sharks in the world. This book is about the great white shark.

This is a whale shark. Whale sharks live in warm waters all over the world. They are one of only two kinds of sharks that grow larger than great white sharks.

How good a name is great white shark? These big animals are certainly sharks. Like most sharks, great whites use five pairs of gills to breathe. They have two fins on their backs. These are called dorsal fins. Great whites also have pairs of fins on their chests that help them steer. These are called pectoral fins.

Great white sharks have fins on their backs and chests. They also have five pairs of gills. The gills are slits on the side of the shark.

Great white sharks are some of the biggest animals in the ocean.

Are great white sharks great? One meaning of *great* is big. Great white sharks are very big. They can grow to more than 20 feet long. They can weigh more than 5,000 pounds. That's heavier than a car!

The great white shark gets its name from its white belly.

Are great white sharks white? Only their bellies are white. Their backs and sides are gray. But when a shark swims under a boat, it sometimes rolls over on its side. Then the people in the boat can see the shark's white belly. This is where the shark got the *white* part of its name.

Great white sharks live in saltwater oceans. Rivers and lakes are freshwater. Some species of sharks can live in freshwater. But great white sharks must live in salty oceans.

These are bull sharks. Bull sharks can live in freshwater for a while.

Great white sharks live in oceans all over the world. People most often see great white sharks in the waters near California, South Africa, and Australia.

These people are watching great white sharks in the waters near South Africa.

Sharks have streamlined bodies.

Great white sharks are born to swim. They have cone-shaped noses and streamlined bodies. Streamlined bodies are rounded and flowing. They travel quickly through ocean waters.

Sharks use their tails to move through the water.

Great white sharks have very powerful tails. The tails are shaped like the letter C. Sharks move their tails from side to side. This helps drive their bodies through the ocean.

Sharks use their dorsal fins to swim straight. They use their winglike pectoral fins to dive and climb, like an airplane.

14

Great white sharks have sharp teeth in their mouths. When they bite, they use about 50 teeth. Shark teeth are shaped like triangles. The edges of the teeth are serrated (ser-ATE-ed). Serrated edges are notched and good for slicing. They help sharks eat meat.

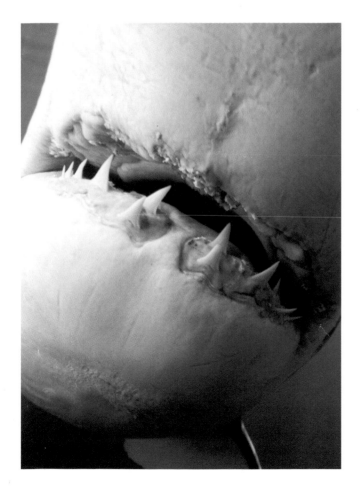

Great white sharks have very sharp teeth.

A great white shark's teeth are arranged in bands. Bands are shaped like horseshoes. A band stretches from one corner of the mouth to the other. A shark has many bands of teeth.

A shark's teeth stretch from one corner of the mouth to the other.

This man is holding the jaws of a great white shark.

Like all sharks, great white sharks often lose their teeth. New teeth take their place. A great white shark does not lose one tooth at a time. Instead, a band of new teeth pushes the band of old teeth forward. The old teeth loosen and fall off. The new band of sharp teeth replaces the old, duller band.

This fossil tooth is from a species of shark that is no longer alive.

What happens to all the teeth that fall out of a shark's mouth? They sink to the bottom of the ocean. After millions of years, they change into rocky copies of the shark's teeth. These rocky copies are called fossils.

Scientists learn a lot about sharks from fossil teeth. They learn about shark species that are no longer alive. By studying the sizes and shapes of fossil teeth, scientists find out how big sharks used to be and what they may have eaten.

The dark tooth is a fossil tooth from an ancient shark. The white tooth is from a great white shark. How big do you think the ancient shark was?

Chapter 2

Great white sharks hunt and eat other animals. What animals do great white sharks eat?

Finding Food

Great white sharks are predators (PREH-duh-turz). Predators are animals that hunt and eat other animals. The animals a predator eats are called prey.

A young great white shark eats fish. An adult eats seals and whales. Adult great white sharks attack and eat elephant seals. Some elephant seals are as big as the sharks that attack them!

This is a northern elephant seal. Great white sharks eat elephant seals.

A great white shark uses its senses to find prey. It can smell seals from far away. It can hear seals swim through the water.

Great white sharks have an excellent sense of smell.

Great white sharks have good eyesight.

As it gets closer to the seals, a shark uses its good eyes to choose the seal it will attack. Sometimes a great white shark may mistake a surfer or swimmer for a seal. But sharks do not usually attack people.

The faces and heads of great white sharks are covered with tiny pores.

Great white sharks use another special sense to find prey. Their faces and heads are covered with tiny holes called pores. The pores help them sense when other animals are near. The muscles of all animals give off small electric shocks. Sharks use their pores to feel these small shocks. When a shark is close to a fish or seal, it can sense the prey's muscles moving. Then the shark knows where to bite.

When a shark attacks a seal, it swims at the seal very quickly. It bumps the seal hard and bites at the same time. The shark's high-speed bump and slashing bite hurt the seal. But strong seals can fight back with their sharp claws. So the shark swims away for a while. It waits for the seal to bleed and weaken. After waiting for a few minutes, the shark moves in to eat.

This great white shark is attacking a seal.

Chapter 3

Great white sharks are always looking for food. Why don't they hunt with other sharks?

Lone Travelers

Great white sharks do not usually swim with other sharks. They almost always hunt by themselves. A great white shark prefers to eat alone.

Like all sharks, great white sharks compete with one another for meals. A small shark will sometimes hunt the same animal as a big shark. But the big shark will chase the small shark and try to make it leave.

Great white sharks will fight one another for food.

Some great white sharks travel long distances. They swim thousands of miles to islands in the middle of the ocean. Then they return to the coastline. Sometimes great white sharks swim near the surface of the water. Sometimes they dive a half mile deep.

This great white shark is swimming near the surface of the water.

Diver Michael Rutzen with a great white shark. Great white sharks can swim faster than people can.

Great white sharks can make their bodies warm even in cold water. A white shark's blood flows through its body and warms its muscles. In this special way, the shark can keep its body warmer than the ocean water. Because the shark's body is warm, the shark swims faster too.

Chapter 4

This is a baby great white shark. What are baby sharks called?

Shark Pups

 Newborn sharks are called pups. A group of pups born at the same time to a mother shark is called a litter. Great white shark mothers may have five to ten pups in a litter.

When a great white shark is ready to have her pups, she swims to a place where there are few large sharks. She has her pups, and then she leaves them behind. She swims back to the place where she usually eats.

Great white sharks do not form families.

Great white shark pups are not like baby dogs. Puppies are helpless. The mother dog must feed and care for them. But shark pups are on their own from the second they are born.

This baby great white shark is exploring the waters on its own.

Great white shark pups start hunting right away. They hunt fish such as salmon. When the pups grow large enough, they hunt seals and sea lions. They compete with other great white sharks for places to hunt.

These are salmon. Baby great white sharks eat salmon.

In about four years, a young white shark grows to about 8 feet long. Fifteen years later, it will be about 18 feet long. Then it is ready to have babies of its own.

When a great white shark is full grown, it is able to have babies.

Chapter 5

Great white sharks swam in oceans millions of years ago. What is the biggest danger sharks face?

Great White Sharks in Danger

Great white sharks have been around for millions of years. Sharks swam in the oceans before humans walked on earth. But sharks face many dangers. The biggest danger to sharks is people.

Long ago, people in Hawaii hunted sharks. They wanted the sharks' teeth. The people used these teeth to make cutting tools and weapons. Some very special tools were made from shark teeth. Hawaiian kings treasured the tools.

These Hawaiian weapons are made of shark teeth.

In most parts of the world, people cannot hunt sharks anymore. It is against the law because sharks are endangered. Endangered animals are animals that might die out forever. But people do hurt sharks by making the ocean water dirty. People make the water dirty by filling it with chemicals. Chemicals can harm sharks.

These workers are cleaning up an oil spill. Sometimes oil leaks out of ships in the ocean. There are chemicals in oil. The chemicals can harm ocean life.

Fishing can harm sharks too. Some people use long lines with sharp hooks to catch fish. Great white sharks sometimes get caught on these lines. Then the sharks get hurt.

Sharks sometimes swallow the bait they find on long fishing lines.

Some people visit the ocean to learn more about great white sharks.

But people are learning to be more responsible. We can take better care of great white sharks when we learn more about them. You are helping to care for great white sharks just by reading this book. Another way to care for sharks is by studying them up close. One way to study sharks is to visit the ocean.

*This diver is studying a great white shark from inside
a cage. The cage protects the diver from the shark.*

It is fun to watch sharks in the ocean, but
it is not always easy. People can see great
whites only when the animals swim near the
water's surface. People sometimes dive with
sharks to watch them more closely. But diving
with sharks can be risky. Sharks may not know
that divers mean to be helpful. They may
mistake a diver for a seal and attack.

The safest way to see a shark up close is by visiting an aquarium. The Monterey Bay aquarium in Monterey, California, is the only aquarium with a great white shark on display. But someday other aquariums will have great white sharks you can visit.

You can see sharks and other ocean life at an aquarium.

There is still a lot to learn about great white sharks. Maybe someday, you can study them. Then you'll know even more about this amazing animal and how it lives.

Many people enjoy studying the great white shark.

Would you like to study sharks someday?

On Sharing a Book

As you know, adults greatly influence a child's attitude toward reading. When a child sees you read, or when you share a book with a child, you're sending a message that reading is important. Show the child that reading a book together is important to you. Find a comfortable, quiet place. Turn off the television and limit other distractions, such as telephone calls.

Be prepared to start slowly. Take turns reading parts of this book. Stop and talk about what you're reading. Talk about the photographs. You may find that much of the shared time is spent discussing just a few pages. This discussion time is valuable for both of you, so don't move through the book too quickly. If the child begins to lose interest, stop reading. Continue sharing the book at another time. When you do pick up the book again, be sure to revisit the parts you have already read. Most importantly, enjoy the book!

Be a Vocabulary Detective

You will find a word list on page 5. Words selected for this list are important to the understanding of the topic of this book. Encourage the child to be a word detective and search for the words as you read the book together. Talk about what the words mean and how they are used in the sentence. Do any of these words have more than one meaning? You will find these words defined in a glossary on page 46.

What about Questions?

Use questions to make sure the child understands the information in this book. Here are some suggestions:

What did this paragraph tell us? What does this picture show? What do you think we'll learn about next? Where do great white sharks live? Could a great white shark live in your backyard? Why/Why not? What do great white sharks eat? How do they get their food? How have humans hurt great white sharks? What are baby great white sharks called? What do you think it's like being a great white shark? What is your favorite part of the book? Why?

If the child has questions, don't hesitate to respond with questions of your own, such as What do *you* think? Why? What is it that you don't know? If the child can't remember certain facts, turn to the index.

Introducing the Index

The index is an important learning tool. It helps readers get information quickly without searching throughout the whole book. Turn to the index on page 47. Choose an entry, such as *pups*, and ask the child to use the index to find out about pups. Repeat this exercise with as many entries as you like. Ask the child to point out the differences between an index and a glossary. (The index helps readers find information quickly, while the glossary tells readers what words mean.)

Where in the World?

Many plants and animals found in the Early Bird Nature Books series live in parts of the world other than the United States. Encourage the child to find the places mentioned in this book on a world map or globe. Take time to talk about climate, terrain, and how you might live in such places.

All the World in Metric!

Although our monetary system is in metric units (based on multiples of 10), the United States is one of the few countries in the world that does not use the metric system of measurement. Here are some conversion activities you and the child can do using a calculator:

WHEN YOU KNOW:	MULTIPLY BY:	TO FIND:
miles	1.609	kilometers
feet	0.3048	meters
inches	2.54	centimeters
gallons	3.785	liters
tons	0.907	metric tons
pounds	0.454	kilograms

Activities

The teeth of great white sharks have the shape of a triangle. Draw some triangles on a sheet of paper. How many different kinds can you draw? Draw one with each side the same length. Draw one with each side a different length. Do they look different? Can you make a triangle shape with paper but without drawing a line? (Hint: fold the paper a few times.)

Feel your teeth with your fingers. What shape are they? Do you think they are as sharp as the teeth of a great white shark? What do people use when their food is too tough to bite with their teeth?

Glossary

bands: rows or strips. A great white shark's teeth are arranged in bands.

compete: to try to win something or do something better than others

dorsal fins: fins on an animal's back

endangered: in danger of dying out forever

fossils: remains, tracks, or traces of an animal that lived long ago

gills: parts of the body used to breathe underwater

litter: a group of babies born at the same time to a mother shark

pectoral fins: fins on an animal's chest

pores: tiny holes. A great white shark uses pores to sense when other animals are near.

predators (PREH-duh-turz): animals that hunt and eat other animals

prey: animals that are hunted and eaten by other animals

pups: baby sharks

serrated (ser-ATE-ed): having an edge with small notches like a saw

streamlined: rounded and flowing

Index

Pages listed in **bold** type refer to photographs.

About the Author

Marine biologist Leighton Taylor began studying the sea while fishing as a small boy in California. He went to graduate school in Hawaii. Hawaii's warm water, bright fish, and coral reefs convinced him to spend his life studying and writing about the animals that live in the sea. He earned a Ph.D. at Scripps Institution of Oceanography. He loves to dive and has made many expeditions in the Pacific Ocean, the Indian Ocean, and the Caribbean Sea. He has discovered and named several new species of sharks, including the deep-sea megamouth shark.